To Our Readers

Changes: Readers of this publication are encouraged to submit suggestions and changes that will improve it. Recommendations may be sent directly to Commanding General, Marine Corps Combat Development Command, Doctrine Division (C 42), 3300 Russell Road, Suite 318A, Quantico, VA 22134-5021 or by fax to 703-784-2917 (DSN 278-2917) or by E-mail to **morgann@mccdc.usmc.mil**. Recommendations should include the following information:

- Location of change
  Publication number and title
  Current page number
  Paragraph number (if applicable)
  Line number
  Figure or table number (if applicable)
- Nature of change
  Add, delete
  Proposed new text, preferably double-spaced and typewritten
- Justification and/or source of change

Additional copies: A printed copy of this publication may be obtained from Marine Corps Logistics Base, Albany, GA 31704-5001, by following the instructions in MCBul 5600, *Marine Corps Doctrinal Publications Status.* An electronic copy may be obtained from the Doctrine Division, MCCDC, world wide web home page which is found at the following universal reference locator: **http://www.doctrine.usmc.mil**.

Unless otherwise stated, whenever the masculine gender is used, both men and women are included.

DEPARTMENT OF THE NAVY
United States Marine Corps
Washington, DC 20380-1775

29 August 2001

FOREWORD

PURPOSE

Marine Corps Reference Publication (MCRP) 3-31B, *Amphibious Ships and Landing Craft Data Book*, is for use in planning where generalized capabilities and measurements are required. In planning for operations where exact capabilities and figures are required, the individual ship's loading characteristics pamphlet (SLCP) must be consulted.

SCOPE

The information contained in this MCRP was obtained from the individual SLCPs and from the Naval Sea Systems Command. The data is based on class averages. No broken stowage factors have been applied to square footage in embarked landing craft.

SUPERSESSION

This book supersedes Fleet Marine Force Reference Publication (FMFRP) 1-18, *Amphibious Ships and Landing Craft Data Book*, dated 6 August 1991.

CERTIFICATION

Reviewed and approved this date.

BY DIRECTION OF THE COMMANDANT OF THE MARINE CORP

EDWARD HANLON, JR.
Lieutenant General, U.S. Marine Corps
Commanding General
Marine Corps Combat Development Command

DISTRIBUTION: 144 000103 00

Contents

Amphibious Command Ship
USS Blue Ridge (LCC-19) Class

***USS Mount Whitney* (LCC-20) Pictured**

Mission

The assigned mission of the amphibious command ship (LCC) is to function as the command ship for a joint task force as the command, control, communications, computers, and intelligence (C4I) platform, or for a naval component commander; numbered fleet commander; commander, amphibious task force (CATF); Marine expeditionary force (MEF).

General Comments

This ship is designed primarily to fulfill command and control requirements for surface, subsurface, and air units engaged in amphibious assaults.

The *USS Blue Ridge* (LCC-19) is distinctive in appearance. The ship can communicate in frequency ranges from high frequency to super high frequency, including two satellite systems for high speed/high volume communication links. The various internal command areas are highly automated to monitor and process information regarding the progress of an amphibious operation. This is the only class of ship designed from its hull up to support the command and control needs of the CATF; commander, landing force (CLF); and tactical air control center (TACC).

General Information

Length (overall)	620 feet
Beam	180 feet
Displacement (light load)	16,100 tons
Displacement (full load)	18,646 tons
Draft (full load)	29 feet
Main engine (geared turbine)	1
Boilers	2
Shaft	1
Shaft horsepower	22,000
Speed	23 knots
Range at 16 knots	13,000 nautical miles
Staff accommodations	217
Crew accommodations	774
Ship's chaplain	Yes

Landing Force Lift General Information

Officer accommodations	56
Enlisted accommodations (E-7)	42
Enlisted accommodations (E-6 and below)	111
Vehicle square	3,015 square feet
Cargo cube	2,175 cubic feet
Helicopter landing spot	1
JP-5	123,510 gallons

Command and Control Systems

Combat Information Center	Yes
Integrated Tactical Amphibious Warfare Data System	No
Ship's Signals Exploitation Space	Yes
Flag Plot	Yes
Landing Force Operations Center	Yes
Joint Intelligence Center	Yes
Supporting Arms Coordination Center	Yes

Command and Control Systems (Continued)

Tactical-Logistical Group	No
Helicopter Logistics Support Group	Yes
Helicopter Direction Center	Yes
Helicopter Coordination Section	Yes
Tactical Air Control Center	Yes

Organic Craft

Landing craft, personnel, large (LCPL)	2
Utility boat	1

Weapons

Phalanx Close-in Weapon System (CIWS)
MK-38 25mm Machine Gun
M-2 .50 caliber Heavy Machine Gun (HMG)
MK-36 Chaff Rocket Super Rapid Booming Offboard Chaff (SRBOC) Launcher

Ships in Class

Hull Number	Ship's Name	Home Port
LCC-19	USS Blue Ridge	Yokosuka, Japan
LCC-20	USS Mount Whitney	Norfolk, VA

Amphibious Assault Ship (General Purpose)
USS Tarawa (LHA-1) Class

USS Nassau (LHA-4) Pictured

Mission

The assigned mission of the amphibious assault ship (general purpose) (LHA) is to embark, deploy, and land elements of a Marine landing force in an amphibious assault by helicopters, landing craft, amphibious vehicles, and by combinations of these methods.

General Comments

The LHA features include a full length flight deck, a landing craft docking well (well deck), large storage areas for vehicles and cargo, and troop berthing for a reinforced battalion. An Integrated Tactical Amphibious Warfare Data System (ITAWDS) provides computerized support in control of helicopters, aircraft, shipboard weapons, sensors, navigation, landing craft, and electronic warfare.

The flag spaces are designed to support the staff of the embarked Navy organization (amphibious squadron [PHIBRON] or an amphibious group [PHIBGRU] staff) and the Marine landing force staff (Marine expeditionary unit [MEU], Marine expeditionary brigade [MEB] or Marine expeditionary force [MEF]). The design of the LHA provides an optimum operational environment for ship's company, embarked staffs, troops, and support personnel prior to, during, and after an amphibious operation.

General Information

Length (overall)	820 feet
Beam	106 feet
Displacement (light load)	33,536 tons
Displacement (full load)	39,967 tons
Draft (full load)	26 feet
Main engines (geared turbine)	2
Boilers	2
Shafts	2
Shaft horsepower	70,000
Speed	24 knots
Range at 20 knots	10,000 nautical miles
Bow thruster	Yes
Staff accommodations	87
Crew accommodations	956
Ship's chaplain	Yes

Landing Force Lift General Information

Officer accommodations	172
Enlisted accommodations (E-7)	59
Enlisted accommodations (E-6 and below)	1,672
Surge accommodations	No
Vehicle square	28,700 square feet
Cargo cube	156,000 cubic feet
Helicopter landing spots	9
Operational CH-46 equivalents	43
JP-5	407,600 gallons
Motor gasoline (MOGAS) (embarked bladder)	500 gallons
Landing force operational reserve material (LFORM)	Yes

Command and Control Systems

Combat Information Center	Yes
Integrated Tactical Amphibious Warfare Data System	Yes
Ship's Signals Exploitation Space	Yes
Flag Plot	Yes
Landing Force Operations Center	Yes
Joint Intelligence Center	Yes
Supporting Arms Coordination Center	Yes
Tactical-Logistical Group	Yes
Helicopter Logistics Support Group	Yes
Tactical Air Control Center	Yes
Helicopter Direction Center	Yes
Helicopter Coordination Section	Yes

Medical Capabilities

Operating rooms	4
Post-operative recovery/Intensive care	17 beds
Isolation ward	4 beds
Primary care ward	48 beds
Ship's doctor	Yes
Ship's dentist	Yes

Well Deck

The landing craft numbers listed below are the maximum number of each type of craft that can be stowed in the well deck exclusive of any other craft. Combinations of these craft may be stowed in the well deck.

Length (to island)	107 feet, 7 inches
Length (overall)	249 feet, 8 inches
Width	76 feet
Height	26 feet, 8 inches
LCAC	1
Landing craft, utility (LCU)	4

Cargo Handling Equipment

Forklift (electric/4-ton)	1
Forklifts (diesel/6-ton)	8
Forklifts (rough terrain/10,000 pounds)	2
Aircraft tow tractors (4¼-ton)	6
Aircraft spotting dollies (6-ton)	3
Aircraft elevators (40-ton aft/ 20-ton portside)	2
Longitudinal pallet conveyor	1
Monorails (2 hooks, each with 3-ton capacity)	3

Organic Craft

LCPL	2

Weapons

Phalanx Close-in Weapon System (CIWS)
Rolling Airframe Missile (RAM) System
MK-36 Chaff Rocket Super Rapid Booming Offboard Chaff (SRBOC) Launcher
MK-38 25mm Machine Gun
M-2 .50 caliber Heavy Machine Gun (HMG)

Ships in Class

Hull Number	Ship's Name	Home Port
LHA-1	USS Tarawa	San Diego, CA
LHA-2	USS Saipan	Norfolk, VA
LHA-3	USS Belleau Wood	San Diego, CA
LHA-4	USS Nassau	Norfolk, VA
LHA-5	USS Peleliu	San Diego, CA

Amphibious Assault Ship (Multipurpose) *USS Wasp* (LHD-1) Class

USS Essex (LHD-2) Pictured

Mission

The assigned mission of the amphibious assault ship (multipurpose) (LHD) is to embark, deploy, and land elements of a Marine landing force in an amphibious assault by helicopters, landing craft, amphibious vehicles, and by combinations of these methods. The LHD is assigned a secondary mission of sea control and power projection in which additional fixed-wing vertical/short takeoff and landing (V/STOL) aircraft and helicopters are deployed.

General Comments

The LHD incorporates the original design features of the LHA. The ship can embark a large segment of a landing force with its equipment and supplies. The flag spaces are designed to support the staff of the embarked Navy organization (amphibious squadron [PHIBRON] or an amphibious group [PHIBGRU] staff) and the Marine landing force staff (Marine expeditionary unit [MEU], Marine expeditionary brigade [MEB]) or Marine expeditionary force [MEF]). An expanded and combined flag data display uses the latest in technology to enhance the commander's ability to control air, land, and sea assets.

The aviation facilities are capable of supporting a composite helicopter squadron or an AV-8B V/STOL squadron or combination of the two. When in its secondary mission, the flight deck can accommodate 20 AV-8B and 4 to 6 SH-60B (LAMPS III), thus enabling the commander to control the sea while projecting power.

General Information

Length (overall)	844 feet
Beam	107 feet
Displacement (light load)	26,840 tons
Displacement (full load)	40,532 tons
Draft (full load)	26 feet, 6 inches
Main engines	2
Boilers	2
Shafts	2
Shaft horsepower	70,000
Speed	22 knots

General Information (Continued)

Bow thruster	No
Staff accommodations	35
Crew accommodations	1,231
Ship's chaplain	Yes

Landing Force Lift General Information

Officer accommodations	173
Enlisted accommodations (E-7)	64
Enlisted accommodations (E-6 and below)	1,656
Surge accommodations (officer)	19
Surge accommodations (E-7)	6
Surge accommodations (E-6 and below)	186
Vehicle square	24,012 square feet
Cargo cube	145,000 cubic feet
Helicopter landing spots	9
Operational CH-46 equivalents	42
JP-5	484,000 gallons
MOGAS (embarked bladder)	500 gallons
LFORM	Yes

Command and Control Systems

Combat Information Center	Yes
Integrated Tactical Amphibious Warfare Data System	Yes
Ship's Signals Exploitation Space	Yes
Flag Plot	Yes

Command and Control Systems (Continued)

Landing Force Operations Center	Yes
Joint Intelligence Center	Yes
Supporting Arms Coordination Center	Yes
Tactical-Logistical Group	Yes
Helicopter Logistics Support Group	Yes
Tactical Air Control Center	Yes
Helicopter Direction Center	Yes
Helicopter Coordination Section	Yes

Medical Capabilities

Operating rooms	6
Post-operative recovery/Intensive care	18 beds
Isolation ward	6 beds
Primary care ward	36 beds
Ship's doctor	Yes
Ship's dentist	Yes

Well Deck

The landing craft numbers listed below are the maximum number of each type of craft that can be stowed in the well deck exclusive of any other craft. Combinations of these craft may be stowed in the well deck.

Length (overall)	322 feet
Width	50 feet
Height	28 feet
LCACs	3
LCUs	2

Cargo Handling Equipment

Forklifts (electric 2-ton)	10
Forklifts (diesel 3-ton)	25

Cargo Handling Equipment (Continued)

Forklifts (rough terrain/10,000 pounds)	2
Aircraft tow tractors	5
Spotting dollies	4
Aircraft elevators (port/starboard 37½-ton)	2
Aircraft crash crane (ACC) (35-ton maximum capability)	1
Monorail (1½-ton)	5
Cargo elevators (6-ton)	6
Pallet conveyors (½-ton/300 pallets per hour)	2

Organic Craft

LCPL	1
7-meter rigid hull inflatable boat (RHIB)	1

Weapons

Phalanx Close-in Weapon System (CIWS)
NATO Sea Sparrow Missile System (NSSMS)

Weapons (Continued)

M-2 .50 caliber Heavy Machine Gun (HMG)
MK-38 25mm Machine Gun
Rolling Airframe Missile (RAM) System

Ships in Class

Hull Number	Ship's Name	Home Port
LHD-1	USS Wasp	Norfolk, VA
LHD-2	USS Essex	Sasebo, Japan
LHD-3	USS Kearsarge	Norfolk, VA
LHD-4	USS Boxer	San Diego, CA
LHD-5	USS Bataan	Norfolk, VA
LHD-6	USS Bon Homme Richard	San Diego, CA
LHD-7	USS Iwo Jima	Norfolk, VA
LHD-8	(Name/delivery date TBD)	TBD

Amphibious Transport Dock
USS Austin (LPD-4)Class

USS Trenton (LPD-14) Pictured

Mission

The assigned mission of the LPD is to transport and land troops and their essential equipment and supplies in an amphibious assault by means of embarked landing craft or amphibious vehicles augmented by helicopter lift.

General Comments

The LPD is a general purpose amphibious ship with substantial lift capacities for troops, vehicles, landing craft, cargo, and bulk fuel. The LPD is capable of ballasting to permit loading and launching of landing craft and assault amphibious vehicles. Vehicles can move about the various decks by a series of power-operated ramps. The well deck can accommodate all types of landing craft currently in the amphibious force inventory. A limited number of helicopters may be transported on the flight deck as the LPD serves as a helicopter platform for landing embarked troops and their supplies. It also serves as a refueling station for helicopters of the landing force. Troops, vehicles, and equipment can be loaded/off-loaded by helicopter and landing craft simultaneously. Several LPDs are flag configured for MEU and PHIBRON size staffs.

General Information

Length (overall)	570 feet
Beam	84 feet
Displacement (light load)	9,128 tons
Displacement (full load)	16,905 tons
Draft (full load)	23 feet
Main engines	2
Boilers	2
Shafts	2
Shaft horsepower	24,000
Speed	21 knots
Range at 20 knots	7,700 nautical miles
Bow thruster	No
Staff accommodations (flag configured only)	60
Crew accommodations	492
Ship's chaplain	Yes

Landing Force Lift General Information

Officer accommodations	68
Enlisted accommodations (E-7)	21
Enlisted accommodations (E-6 and below)	620
Surge accommodations (E-6 and below)	176
Vehicle square	14,000 square feet
Cargo cube	51,000 cubic feet
Helicopter landing spots	2
Operational CH-46 equivalents	4
JP-5	288,700 gallons
MOGAS	21,900 gallons
LFORM	Yes

Organic Craft

Utility boat	1
LCPL	2
7-meter RHIB	1

Command and Control Systems

Combat Information Center	Yes
Integrated Tactical Amphibious Warfare Data System	No
Ship's Signals Exploitation Space (flag configured only)	Yes
Flag Plot (flag configured only)	Yes

Command and Control Systems (Continued)

Troop Operations and Logistics Center	Yes
Joint Intelligence Center	No
Supporting Arms Coordination Center (flag configured only)	Yes
Tactical-Logistical Group	No
Helicopter Logistics Support Group	No
Tactical Air Control Center	No
Helicopter Direction Center	No
Helicopter Coordination Section	Yes

Medical Capabilities

Operating room	1
Post-operative recovery/Intensive care	No
Isolation ward	4 beds
Primary care ward	8 beds
Casualty overflow	No
Ship's doctor	Yes
Ship's dentist	Yes

Cargo Handling Equipment

Forklifts (electric/2-ton)	10
Forklifts (rough terrain/6,000 pounds)	2
Cargo and weapons elevator (8-ton)	1
Pallet conveyors(1½-ton)	3
Monorails (2 hooks, each with 2-ton capacity)	2
Boat and aircraft crane (30-ton)	1

Well Deck

The landing craft numbers listed below are the maximum number of each type of craft that can be stowed in the well deck exclusive of any other craft. Combinations of these craft may be stowed in the well deck.

Length (overall)	168 feet
Width	50 feet
Height	20 feet
LCAC	1
LCU	1

Weapons

Phalanx Close-in Weapon system (CIWS)
MK-36 Chaff Rocket Super Rapid Booming Offboard Chaff (SRBOC) Launcher

Ships in Class

Hull Number	Ship's Name	Home Port	Flag Configured
LPD-4	USS Austin	Norfolk, VA	No
LPD-5	USS Ogden	San Diego, CA	No
LPD-6	USS Duluth	San Diego, CA	No
LPD-7	USS Cleveland	San Diego, CA	Yes
LPD-8	USS Dubuque	San Diego, CA	Yes
LPD-9	USS Denver	San Diego, CA	Yes
LPD-10	USS Juneau	Sasebo, Japan	Yes
LPD-12	USS Shreveport	Norfolk, VA	Yes
LPD-13	USS Nashville	Norfolk, VA	Yes
LPD-14	USS Trenton	Norfolk, VA	No
LPD-15	USS Ponce	Norfolk, VA	No

Amphibious Transport Dock
USS San Antonio (LPD-17) Class

***USS San Antonio* (LPD-17) Pictured**

Mission

The assigned mission of the LPD-17 class ships is to embark, transport, and land elements of the landing force in an assault by helicopters, landing craft, amphibious assault vehicles, and by a combination of these methods.

General Comments

The San Antonio class LPD will provide greatly improved warfighting capabilities including an advanced command and control suite, a greatly increased lift capacity, including substantial increases in vehicle and cargo carrying capability, and advanced ship survivability features. These ships have been designed from the keel up to support the Marine Corps 'mobility triad'—the landing craft air cushion (LCAC) vehicle, advanced amphibious assault vehicle (AAAV), and MV-22 (Osprey tiltrotor aircraft)—making this class a key element of 21st century amphibious ready groups. It is also certified for the AV-8B aircraft. The LPD-17 class ships are scheduled to replace the older LPD-4 class.

The San Antonio class design integrates the latest in command, control, communications, computers, intelligence, surveillance and reconnaissance (C4ISR) capability. These capabilities are further enhanced by

additional, dedicated intelligence, mission planning, and command and control spaces. The shipboard wide area network (SWAN) developed for LPD-17 is a fiber optic shipwide large area computer network.

General Information

Length (overall)	684 feet
Beam	105 feet
Displacement (full load)	25,296 tons
Draft (full load)	23 feet
Main engines	4
Boilers	2
Shafts	2
Speed	22+ knots
Bow thruster	No
Staff accommodations	No
Crew accommodations	493
Ship's chaplain	Yes

Landing Force Lift General Information

Officer accommodations	66
Enlisted accommodations (E-7)	41
Enlisted accommodations (E-6 and below)	597
Surge accommodations (officer)	11
Surge accommodations (E-7)	6
Surge accommodations (E-6 and below)	78
Vehicle square	25,000 square feet
Cargo cube	35,000 cubic feet
Helicopter landing spots	2
Operational CH-46 equivalents	4
JP-5	215,000 gallons
MOGAS	10,000 gallons
LFORM	Yes

Organic Craft

LCPL	1
7-meter RHIBs	2

Command and Control Systems

Combat Information Center	Yes
Integrated Tactical Amphibious Warfare Data System	No
Ship's Signals Exploitation Space	Yes
Troop Operations and Logistics Center	Yes

Command and Control Systems (Continued)

Joint Intelligence Center	Yes
Supporting Arms Coordination Center	Yes
Tactical-Logistical Group	Yes
Helicopter Logistics Support Group	No
Tactical Air Control Center	No
Helicopter Direction Center	No
Helicopter Coordination Section	Yes

Medical Capabilities

Operating rooms	2
Post-operative recovery/Intensive care	No
Isolation ward	4 beds
Primary care ward	24 beds
Ship's doctor	Yes
Ship's dentist	Yes

Cargo Handling Equipment

Forklifts (electric/2-ton)	10
Forklifts (rough terrain/6,000 pounds)	2
Cargo and weapons elevator (8-ton)	1
Pallet conveyors (1½-ton)	3
Monorails (2 hooks, each with 2-ton capacity)	6
Boat and aircraft crane (30-ton)	1

Well Deck

The landing craft numbers listed below are the maximum number of each type of craft that can be stowed in the well deck exclusive of any other craft. Combinations of these craft may be stowed in the well deck.

Length (overall)	188 feet
Width	50 feet
Height	31 feet
LCAC	2
LCU	1
LCM-8	4

Weapons

MK -41, 16 Cell Vertical Launch System (VLS) space and weight only
MK-144 Mod 0 Rolling Air Frame Missile (RAM) Launchers
MK-26 .50 caliber Machine Guns
MK-46 Mod 1 30mm Machine Gun

Ships in Class

Hull Number	Ship's Name	Home Port	Scheduled Delivery
LPD-17	USS San Antonio	Norfolk, VA	11/04
LPD-18	USS New Orleans	San Diego, CA	07/05
LPD-19	USS Mesa Verde	Norfolk, VA	10/05
LPD-20	USS Green Bay	San Diego, CA	03/06
LPD-21	TBD	San Diego, CA	11/06
LPD-22	TBD	San Diego, CA	04/07
LPD-23	TBD	Sasebo, Japan	07/07
LPD-24	TBD	San Diego, CA	03/08
LPD-25	TBD	Norfolk, VA	10/08
LPD-26	TBD	Norfolk, VA	01/09
LPD-27	TBD	Norfolk, VA	09/09
LPD-28	TBD	Norfolk, VA	08/10

Dock Landing Ship
USS Anchorage (LSD-36) Class

USS Mount Vernon (LSD-39) Pictured

Mission

The assigned mission of the LSD-36 is to transport and launch loaded amphibious craft and vehicles with their crews and embarked personnel in amphibious assaults by landing craft and amphibious vehicles. It can render limited docking repair service to small ships and craft.

General Comments

Major spaces for carrying vehicles and/or cargo or conducting helicopter operations are the helicopter platform, the super deck, the mezzanine deck, and the well deck. The mezzanine deck, super deck, and helicopter platform are constructed so they can be removed and stored ashore should assigned operations dictate. Mezzanine decks are frequently removed, but super decks and helicopter platforms are rarely removed. Vehicles may be loaded via landing craft into the well deck or lifted aboard by crane to the super deck for transit via ramps to other decks for stowage. Vehicles stowed in the well deck should be at least 50 feet forward of any landing craft to minimize potential salt water immersion during ballasting operations.

General Information

Length (overall)	562 feet
Beam	8 4feet
Displacement (light load)	8,200 tons
Displacement (full load)	13,680 tons
Draft (full load)	20 feet
Main engines	2
Boilers	2
Shafts	2
Shaft horsepower	24,000
Speed	22 knots
Range at 12 knots	14,800 nautical miles
Bow thruster	No
Staff accommodations	No
Crew accommodations	426
Ship's chaplain	No

Landing Force Lift General Information

Officer accommodations	25
Enlisted accommodations (E-7)	8
Enlisted accommodations (E-6 and below)	303
Surge accommodations (E-6 and below)	No
Vehicle square (with mezzanine)	19,700 square feet
Vehicle square (without mezzanine)	8,800 square feet
Cargo cube	1,800 cubic feet
Helicopter landing spot	1
Operational CH-46 equivalent	No
JP-5	31,500 gallons
MOGAS	No
LFORM	No

Command and Control Systems

Combat Information Center	Yes
Integrated Tactical Amphibious Warfare Data System	No
Ship's Signals Exploitation Space	No
Flag Plot	No
Landing Force Operations Center	No
Joint Intelligence Center	No
Supporting Arms Coordination Center	No
Tactical-Logistical Group	No
Helicopter Logistics Support Group	No
Tactical Air Control Center	No
Helicopter Direction Center	No
Helicopter Coordination Section	Yes

Medical Capabilities

Operating room	No
Post-operative recovery/Intensive care	1 bed
Isolation ward	2 beds
Primary care ward	8 beds
Casualty overflow	No
Ship's doctor	No
Ship's dentist	Yes

Well Deck

The landing craft numbers listed below are the maximum number of each type of craft that can be stowed in the well deck exclusive of any other craft. Combinations of these craft may be stowed in the well deck.

Length (overall)	436 feet
Width	50 feet
Height	21 feet
LCACs (with mezzanine)	2
LCACs (without mezzanine)	3
LCU (with mezzanine)	1
LCUs (without mezzanine)	3

Cargo Handling Equipment

Forklift (rough terrain/6,000 pounds)	1
Monorails (6-ton)	2
Boat and aircraft crane (20-ton)	1
Boat and aircraft crane (60-ton)	1

Organic Craft

LCPL	2

Weapons

Phalanx Close-in Weapon System (CIWS)
MK-36 Chaff Rocket Super Rapid Booming Offboard Chaff (SRBOC) Launcher

Ships In Class

Hull Number	Ship's Name	Home Port
LSD-36	*USS Anchorage*	San Diego, CA
LSD-37	*USS Portland*	Little Creek, VA
LSD-39	*USS Mount Vernon*	San Diego, CA

Dock Landing Ship
USS Whidbey Island (LSD-41) Class

USS Fort McHenry (LSD-43) Pictured

Mission

The assigned mission of the dock landing ship (LSD-41) is to transport and launch loaded amphibious craft and vehicles with their crews and embarked personnel in amphibious assaults by landing craft and amphibious vehicles. It can render limited docking repair service to small ships and craft.

General Comments

The LSD-41 provides for greater storage space of weapons and equipment, improved facilities for embarked troops, greater range of operations, and the capability to embark either conventional landing craft or LCAC. The ships incorporate materials handling equipment including elevators, package/roller conveyors and forklifts, pallet transporters, and a turntable similar to that found on an LST. The turntable is located between the well deck and the helicopter deck forward of the boat deck to assist in the rapid turnaround of vehicles and equipment during loading/offloading operations.

General Information

Length (overall)	609 feet
Beam	84 feet
Displacement (light load)	10,560 tons
Displacement (full load)	15,165 tons
Draft (full load)	20 feet
Main engines (geared diesel)	4
Boiler	No
Shafts	2
Shaft horsepower	34,000
Speed	20+ knots
Bow thruster	No
Staff accommodations	No
Crew accommodations	413
Ship's chaplain	No

Landing Force Lift General Information

Officer accommodations	27
Enlisted accommodations (E-7)	13
Enlisted accommodations (E-6 and below)	362
Surge accommodations (officer)	7
Surge accommodations (E-7)	7
Surge accommodations (E-6 and below)	88
Vehicle square	11,831 square feet
Cargo cube	8,970 cubic feet
Helicopter landing spots	2
Operational CH-46 equivalent	No
JP-5	53,000 gallons
MOGAS	766 gallons
LFORM	No

Command and Control Systems

Command and control systems on the LSD-41 are designed to support the command, control, communications, computer systems, and intelligence (C4I) requirements for own ship independent operations and in conjunction with an amphibious task force.

Combat Information Center	Yes
Integrated Tactical Amphibious Warfare Data System	No
Ship's Signals Exploitation Space	No
Flag Plot	No
Landing Force Operations Center	No
Joint Intelligence Center	No
Supporting Arms Coordination Center	No
Tactical-Logistical Group	Yes
Helicopter Logistics Support Group	No

Command and Control Systems (Continued)

Tactical Air Control Center	No
Helicopter Direction Center	No
Helicopter Coordination Section	Yes

Medical Capabilities

Operating room	1
Post-operative recovery/Intensive care	1 bed
Isolation ward	2 beds
Primary care ward	5 beds
Casualty overflow	No
Ship's doctor	Yes
Ship's dentist	Yes

Cargo Handling Equipment

Reaching and tiering forklifts (electric/2-ton)	2
Pallet jacks (electric/3-ton)	2
Forklifts (rough terrain/6,000 pounds)	2
Cargo elevator (4-ton)	1
Bridge crane (15-ton [two 7½-ton hoists])	1
Boat and aircraft crane (60-ton)	2
Boat and aircraft crane (20-ton)	1
Turntable	1

Well Deck

The landing craft numbers listed below are the maximum number of each type of craft that can be stowed in the well deck exclusive of any other craft. Combinations of these craft may be stowed in the well deck.

Length (overall)	440 feet
Width	50 feet
Height	27 feet
LCACs	4
LCUs	3

Organic Craft

Utility Boat	1
LCPL	2

Weapons

Phalanx CIWS
MK-38 25mm Machine Gun
Super Rapid Booming Offboard Chaff (SRBOC)
Rolling Airframe Missile (RAM) System

Ships in Class

Hull Number	Ship's Name	Home Port
LSD-41	USS Whidbey Island	Little Creek, VA
LSD-42	USS Germantown	Sasebo, Japan
LSD-43	USS Fort McHenry	San Diego, CA
LSD-44	USS Gunston Hall	Little Creek, VA
LSD-45	USS Comstock	San Diego, CA
LSD-46	USS Tortuga	Little Creek, VA
LSD-47	USS Rushmore	San Diego, CA
LSD-48	USS Ashland	Little Creek, VA

Dock Landing Ship (Cargo Variant)
USS Harpers Ferry (LSD-49) Class

***USS Harpers Ferry* (LSD-49) Pictured**

Mission

The assigned mission of the dock landing ship (LSD-49) is to transport and launch loaded amphibious craft and vehicles with their crews and embarked personnel in amphibious assaults by landing craft and amphibious vehicles. It can render limited docking repair service to small ships and craft.

General Comments

The LSD-49 is the cargo variant (CV) of the LSD-41 ship. Its well deck is shortened to half the length of the LSD-41 to provide space for additional munitions and vehicle stowage. The LSD-49 has stowage space for 18 percent more vehicles and seven times as much stowage space for cargo as the LSD-41. It is not equipped with a well deck bridge crane and is not designed to perform LCAC organizational level maintenance. Its single 30-ton crane can offload only to the starboard side. Intraship, it has 12 forklifts, 3 lift platforms, 2 elevators, and 2 pallet transporters for rapid cargo movement.

General Information

Length (overall)	609 feet
Beam	84 feet
Displacement (light load)	11,328 tons
Displacement (full load)	16,740 tons
Draft (full load)	20 feet
Main engines (geared diesel)	4
Boiler	No
Shafts	2
Shaft horsepower	34,000
Speed	Classified
Range	Classified
Bow thruster	No
Staff accommodations	No
Crew accommodations	413
Ship's chaplain	No

Landing Force Lift General Information

Officer accommodations	27
Enlisted accommodations (E-7)	18
Enlisted accommodations (E-6 and below)	362
Surge accommodations (officer)	7
Surge accommodations (E-7)	6
Surge accommodations (E-6 and below)	88
Vehicle square	20,200 square feet
Cargo cube	67,600 cubic feet
Helicopter landing spots	2
Operational CH-46 equivalent	No
JP-5	50,600 gallons
MOGAS	No
LFORM	Yes

Command and Control Systems

Command and control systems on the LSD-49 (CV) are designed to support the C4I requirements for own ship independent operations and in conjunction with an amphibious task force.

Combat Information Center	Yes
Integrated Tactical Amphibious Warfare Data System	No
Ship's Signals Exploitation Space	No
Flag Plot	No
Landing Force Operations Center	No
Joint Intelligence Center	No
Supporting Arms Coordination Center	No
Tactical-Logistical Group	Yes

Command and Control Systems (Continued)

Helicopter Logistics Support Group	No
Tactical Air Control Center	No
Helicopter Direction Center	No
Helicopter Coordination Section	Yes

Medical Capabilities

Operating Room	1
Post-operative recovery/Intensive care	1 bed
Isolation ward	2 beds
Primary care ward	5 beds
Casualty overflow	No
Ship's doctor	Yes
Ship's dentist	Yes

Cargo Handling Equipment

Forklifts (electric/2-ton)	7
Forklifts (rough terrain/4,000 pounds)	3
Forklifts (rough terrain/6,000 pounds)	2
Cargo lift platforms	3
Cargo elevators (4-ton)	2
Boat and aircraft crane (30-ton)	1
Cargo weapons elevator (12,000 pounds)	1

Well Deck

The landing craft numbers listed below are the maximum number of each type of craft that can be stowed in the well deck exclusive of any other craft. Combinations of these craft may be stowed in the well deck.

Length (overall)	180 feet
Width	50 feet
Height	30 feet
LCACs	2
LCU	1

Organic Craft

Utility Boat	1
LCPL	2

Weapons

Phalanx Close-in Weapon System (CIWS)
25mm Machine Guns
Super Rapid Booming Offboard Chaff (SRBOC)
Rolling Airframe Missile (RAM) System

Ships in Class

Hull Number	Ship's Name	Home Port
LSD-49	*USS Harpers Ferry*	San Diego, CA
LSD-50	*USS Carter Hall*	Little Creek, VA
LSD-51	*USS Oak Hill*	Little Creek, VA
LSD-52	*USS Pearl Harbor*	San Diego, CA

Landing Craft Air Cushion (LCAC)

Mission

The LCAC's mission is to land heavy vehicles, equipment, personnel, and cargo in amphibious assaults.

General Information

The LCAC is the latest generation of amphibious assault landing craft. Combining the heavy lift capacity of the surface assault with high speeds of helicopter-borne assault, the LCAC adds a new dimension to the capabilities of amphibious forces. It is capable of traveling over land and water. At over-the-horizon (OTH) distances of 12 to 100 nautical miles, LCAC offers the military planner another method for attaining surprise when conducting amphibious operations.

The addition of air cushion technology adds high speed and long range to surface-borne amphibious operations. Additional flexibility is provided by LCAC's ability to operate independent of tides and hydrographic constraint. In some cases, the LCAC will have a significant ability to influence operations beyond the high water mark. Weather can affect LCAC operations, but it is less of a factor than for other ship-to-shore delivery means.

Characteristics

Length overall (off cushion)	81 feet
Length overall (on cushion)	87 feet, 11 inches
Width overall (off cushion)	43 feet, 8 inches
Width overall (on cushion)	47 feet
Height (on cushion)	23 feet, 8 inches
Cargo deck length	67 feet
Cargo deck width (maximum)	27 feet
Cargo deck	1,809 square feet
Troop capacity	24
Bow ramp width	28 feet, 4 inches
Bow ramp angle	14 degrees
Stern ramp width	14 feet, 10 inches
Stern ramp angle	14 degrees
Cargo capacity (design)	60 tons
Cargo capacity (overload)	75 tons
Displacement (full load)	166.6 tons
Displacement (capacity load)	181.6 tons
Speed	40+ knots
Range	200 nautical miles
Propulsion (turbo fan 40B gas turbines)	4
Crew	5

Landing Craft Utility (LCU)

Mission

The LCU's mission is to land heavy vehicles, equipment, personnel, and cargo in an amphibious assault.

General Information

The LCU is a highly versatile craft; like others of the landing craft family, it has been adapted for many uses including salvage operations, ferry boats for vehicles and passengers, and underwater test platforms. It is a self-sustaining craft with the typical habitability features found aboard ships. Its welded steel hull provides high durability with deck loads of 800 pounds per square foot. Arrangement of machinery and equipment has taken into account built-in redundancy in the event of battle damage. The craft features two engine rooms separated by a watertight bulkhead to permit limited operation in the event that one engine room is disabled. An anchor system is installed on the starboard side aft to assist in retracting from the beach.

Characteristics

Length (overall)	135 feet
Width (overall)	29 feet, 6 inches
Height (mast folded)	17 feet, 9 inches
Cargo deck length	121 feet
Cargo deck width (maximum)	25 feet
Cargo deck	1,850 square feet
Displacement (loaded)	437 tons
Troop capacity (on deck)	400
Bow ramp width	14 feet, 3 inches
Stern ramp width	18 feet
Cargo capacity	143 tons
Speed	12 knots
Range	1,200 nautical miles
Propulsion (diesel)	2
Draft fore	3 feet, 6 inches
Draft aft	6 foot, 10 inches
Crew	11

Landing Craft Mechanized
LCM Mark 8 (LCM-8)

Mission

The LCM's mission is to land personnel, supplies, and equipment in an amphibious assault or in direct support of maritime prepositioning force operations.

Characteristics	Steel	Aluminum
Length (overall)	73 feet, 7 inches	74 feet, 6 inches
Width (overall)	21 feet, 1 inch	21 feet, 1 inch
Cargo deck length	42 feet	42 feet
Cargo deck width (maximum)	14 feet	17 feet
Cargo deck	588 square feet	714 square feet

Characteristics	Steel	Aluminum
Displacement (loaded)	105 tons	107 tons
Troop capacity	200	200
Bow ramp width	14 feet, 9 inches	14 feet, 9 inches
Cargo capacity	60 tons	60 tons
Speed	12 knots	12 knots
Propulsion (diesel)	2	2
Draft fore	4 feet, 5 inches	3 feet, 10 inches
Draft aft	4 feet, 10 inches	4 feet, 3 inches
Crew (wartime)	5	5
Crew (peacetime)	4	4

APPENDIX: NAVY INACTIVE FLEET

Amphibious Cargo Ship
USS Charleston (LKA-113) Class

***USS El Paso* (LKA-117) Pictured**

NOTE: All five LKAs have been decommissioned and layed up in the Navy Inactive Fleet as mobilization assets (Maintenance Category B) through FY09.

Mission

The assigned mission of the amphibious cargo ship (LKA) is to transport and land combat equipment and material with attendant personnel in an amphibious assault.

General Comments

The *USS Charleston* LKA provides considerable flexibility in cargo stowage methods. The cargo elevators servicing holds 1, 3, and 4 make all categories of supplies and all levels available simultaneously to either the main deck or the helicopter platform. Use of the ship's forklifts and pallet transporters speed the maneuvering of cargo in the holds and enable delivery to various debarkation stations via the main deck passageways, which run the length of the ship. The arrangement and quantity of booms and cargo elevators make it possible to simultaneously embark/debark vehicles and cargo. Vehicles in upper stowage spaces can be embarked/debarked through the hatches with cargo booms, while pallets are embarked/debarked in lower stowage spaces by elevators. The main deck hatch of hold 2 is

unobstructed and can be opened for embarking/debarking of vehicles without the delay of unloading landing craft stowed on the hatch. Hold 4 is well suited for high priority cargo because of its direct access to the flight deck or main deck via elevator number 5.

General Information

Length (overall)	575 feet
Beam	82 feet
Displacement (light load)	10,000 tons
Displacement (full load)	20,700 tons
Draft (full load)	25 feet
Main engine	1
Boilers	2
Shaft	1
Shaft horsepower	19,250
Speed	20 knots
Range at 16 knots	9,600 nautical miles
Bow thruster	No
Staff accommodations	No
Crew accommodations	409
Ship's chaplain	No

Landing Force Lift General Information

Officer accommodations	15
Enlisted accommodations (E-7)	6
Enlisted accommodations (E-6 and below)	205
Surge accommodations (E-6 and below)	No
Vehicle square (square feet)	47,000
Cargo cube (cubic feet)	88,100
Helicopter landing spot	1
Operational CH-46 equivalent	No
JP-5	52,600 gallons
MOGAS	No
LFORM	Yes

Command and Control Systems

Combat Information Center	Yes
Integrated Tactical Amphibious Warfare Data System	No
Ship's Signals Exploitation Space	No
Flag Plot	No
Landing Force Operations Center	No
Joint Intelligence Center	No
Supporting Arms Coordination Center	No
Tactical-Logistical Group	No
Helicopter Logistics Support Group	No
Tactical Air Control Center	No
Helicopter Direction Center	No
Helicopter Coordination Section	Yes

Medical Capabilities

Operating room	1 bed
Post-operative recovery/Intensive care	No
Isolation ward	4 beds
Primary care ward	9 beds
Casualty overflow	No
Ship's doctor	Yes
Ship's dentist	No

Cargo Handling Equipment

Forklifts (electric/2-ton)	10
Forklifts (diesel/3-ton)	2
Pallet jacks (electric/2-ton)	3
Cargo elevators (2-ton)	5
Cargo elevator (6-ton)	1
Booms (15-ton)	8
Booms (40-ton)	2
Booms (70-ton)	2

Organic Craft

LCM-8	4
LCPL	2

Weapons

Phalanx Close-In Weapon System (CIWS), MK-16 20mm
3-in-50 (Twin MK-33)
MK-36 Chaff Rocket Super Rapid Booming Offboard Chaff (SRBOC) Launcher

Ships In Class

Hull Number	Ship's Name	Location
LKA-113	*USS Charleston*	NISMF Philadelphia, PA
PALKA-114	*USS Durham*	NISMF Pearl Harbor, HI
LKA-115	*USS Mobile*	NISMF Philadelphia, PA
PALKA-116	*USS St. Louis*	NISMF Pearl Harbor, HI
HILKA-117	*USS El Paso*	NISMF Philadelphia, PA

Tank Landing Ship
USS Newport (LST-1179) Class

USS La Moure County (LST-1194) Pictured

NOTE: The LSTs listed on page A-6, plus four in the Navy Inactive Fleet (Maintenance Category B), are in support of the Amphibious Lift Enhancement Plan (ALEP) to ensure adequate amphibious lift availability in a crisis. LSTs 1182, 1187, 1190 and 1191 will be retained as mobilization assets until FY09.

Mission

The assigned mission of the LST is to transport and land amphibious assault vehicles, tanks, combat vehicles, and equipment in amphibious assaults.

General Comments

The *USS Newport* LST employs higher speeds and trimmer lines than slower snub-nosed LSTs of World War II. It has a sharper clipper-ship bow topped by two huge derricks used to extend and retract its bow ramp. The 110-foot aluminum ramp has a 75-ton capacity and is extended and retracted by a semiautomatic system of sensing switches that operate power winches below decks. When extended, the ramp is attached to the main deck by a pivot post. The end of the ramp rests on a beach or pontoon causeway, depending on the water depth and the beach gradient. *USS Newport* LST is also the first amphibious ship to be fitted with an internal side propulsion unit located below the waterline in the vicinity of the bow. The bow thruster allows the bow to be pushed from side to side while the stern remains relatively stationary. This increased maneuverability has proven invaluable in restricted waters and especially during mooring and causeway marriages. The first stern gate used on an

LST is found in the *USS Newport* LST and allows loading and launching of amphibious assault vehicles (AAVs) as well as sterngate marriages with landing craft utility (LCU).

General Information

Length (overall)	522 feet
Beam	70 feet
Displacement (light load)	4,975 tons
Displacement (full load)	8,450 tons
Draft (full load)	20 feet
Main engines (diesel)	6
Boilers (150 psi)	2
Shafts	2
Shaft horsepower	16,800
Speed	22 knots
Range	14,250 nautical miles
Bow thruster	Yes
Staff accommodations	No
Crew accommodations	245
Ship's chaplain	No

Landing Force Lift General Information

Officer accommodations	20
Enlisted accommodations (E-7)	21
Enlisted accommodations (E-6 and below)	273
Surge accommodations (E-6 and Below)	72
Vehicle square	16,500 square feet
Cargo cube	4,500 cubic feet
Helicopter landing spot	1
Operational CH-46 equivalent	No
JP-5	19,100 gallons
MOGAS	7,200 gallons
LFORM	No

Command and Control Systems

Combat Information Center	Yes
Integrated Tactical Amphibious Warfare Data System	No
Ship's Signals Exploitation Space	No
Flag Plot	No
Landing Force Operations Center	No
Joint Intelligence Center	No
Supporting Arms Coordination Center	No
Tactical-Logistical Group	No
Helicopter Logistics Support Group	No

Command and Control Systems (Continued)

Tactical Air Control Center	No
Helicopter Direction Center	No
Helicopter Coordination Section	Yes

Organic Craft

LCVPs	3
LCPL	1

Medical Capabilities

Operating room	No
Post-operative recovery/Intensive care	No
Isolation ward	No
Primary care ward	No
Casualty overflow	No
Ship's doctor	No
Ship's dentist	No

Cargo Handling Equipment

Forklifts (diesel/3-ton)	2
Forklift (rough terrain/6,000 pounds)	1
Cargo booms (10-ton)	2
Turntables	2

Weapons

Phalanx Close-in Weapon System (CIWS)
Super Rapid Booming Offboard Chaff (SRBOC)

Ships in Class

Hull Number	Ship's Name	Location
LST-1184	*USS Frederick* (Reserve Fleet)	Pearl Harbor, HI
LST 1182	*USS Fresno*	NISMF Pearl Harbor, HI
LST 1187	*USS Tuscaloosa*	NISMF Pearl Harbor HI
LST 1190	*USS Boulder*	NISMF Philadelphia, PA
LST 1191	*USS Racine*	NISMF Pearl Harbor, HI
LST-1194	*USS La Moure County* (Reserve Fleet)	Little Creek, VA

GLOSSARY

PART 1. ABBREVIATIONS AND ACRONYMS

AAAV . . . . advanced amphibious assault vehicle

ACC . . . . aircraft crash crane

AAV . . . . assault amphibious vehicle

ALEP. . . . . Amphibious Lift Enhancement Plan

C4I. . . . . command, control, communications, computers, and intelligence

C4ISR . . . . command, control, communications, computers, intelligence, surveillance, and reconnaissance

CATF . . . . .commander, amphibious task force

CIC . . . . combat information center

CIWS. . . . . Close-in Weapon System

CLF. . . . . .commander, landing force

CV. . . . . cargo variant

HCS. . . . . helicopter coordination section

HDC . . . . .helicopter direction center

HLSG . . . . .helicopter logistics support group

HMG. heavy machine gun

ITAWDS. . . . . Integrated Tactical Amphibious Warfare Data System

JIC. . . . . .joint intelligence center

JTF . . . . .joint task force

LCAC . . . . landing craft air cushion

LCC. . . . . amphibious command ship

LCM . . . . landing craft mechanized

LCPL. . . . . .landing craft, personnel, large

LCU. . . . . landing craft utility

LCVP . . . . landing craft, vehicle, personnel

LFOC . . . . landing force operations center

LFORM. . . landing force operational reserve material

LHA . . . . . amphibious assault ship (general purpose)

LHD . . . . amphibious assault ship (multipurpose)

LKA . . . . .amphibious cargo ship

LPD. . . . . amphibious transport dock

LSD. . . . . dock landing ship

LST . . . . .tank landing ship

MEB . . . . Marine expeditionary brigade

MEF . . . . .Marine expeditionary force

MEU . . . . .Marine expeditionary unit

mm . . . . millimeter

MOGAS . . . . .motor gasoline

NSSMS . . . . NATO Seasparrow missile system

OTH . . . . over-the-horizon

PHIBGRU. amphibious group

PHIBRON. . . . . .amphibious squadron

psi . . . . pounds per square inch

RAM . . . . Rolling Airframe Missile

RHIB. . . . . rigid hull inflatable boat

RRF. . . . . .Ready Reserve Force

SACC . . . . .supporting arms coordination center

SLCP. . . . . ship's loading characteristics pamphlet

SRBOC . . . . super rapid booming offboard chaff

SSDS. . . . . Ship's Self Defense System

SSES . . . . .ship's signals exploitation space

SWAN. . . . . .shipboard wide area network

TACC . . . . tactical air control center (USN)

TACLOG . . . . .tactical-logistical group

VLS. . . . . vertical launch system

V/STOL. . . . . vertical/short takeoff and landing

PART 2. TERMS AND DEFINITIONS

ballasting operations. Operations conducted by amphibious shipping to flood the ship's well deck allowing landing craft to enter the ship and load or unload personnel, vehicles and cargo. Although this method is time consuming, it is considered the safest method of embarkation.

broken stowage. The space lost in the holds of a vessel because of the contour of the ship and the shape of the cargo. Also, a factor applied to the available space for embarkation due to the loss between boxes, between vehicles, around stanchions, and over cargo. The factor will vary depending on the type and size of vehicles, type and size of general cargo, training and experience of loading personnel, type of loading, method of stowage, and configuration of compartments.

flag spaces. Billeting and office spaces aboard the LHA, LHD, and command configured LPD-4 Class amphibious shipping allocated to the CATF staff.

helicopter platform. A term used for amphibious shipping with the capability to support the landing of helicopters for the purpose of embarking or debarking troops and cargo and for refueling aircraft.

mezzanine deck. Applicable to the LSD-36 Class amphibious ship. A system of 14 portable/removable sections installed between the well deck and the super deck for stowage of vehicles and cargo. When installed, ramps provide vehicle access from the well deck to the super deck and flight deck. Also referred to as "'tween" deck.

MEU (Marine Expeditionary Unit). A Marine air-ground task force that is constructed around an infantry battalion reinforced, a helicopter squadron reinforced, and a task-organized combat service support element. It normally fulfills Marine Corps forward sea-based deployment requirements. The Marine expeditionary unit provides an immediate reaction capability for crisis response and is capable of limited combat operations. Also called MEU.

sterngate marriage. Weather conditions permitting, displacement landing craft are brought to the sterngate, secured, and allowed to lower their bow ramp to a dry well deck. Personnel and vehicles can be quickly loaded or unloaded over the ramp and the need for time-consuming ballasting operations are negated.

super deck. Applicable to the LSD-36 Class amphibious ship. Installed forward of the flight deck, it provides a stowage area for vehicles and cargo and can be accessed from the well deck via the mezzanine deck ramps or lifted aboard using the ship's cranes.